ALPHABETICA

ALPHABETICA

poems

∼

Juliet Mattila

Story Line Press | *Pasadena, CA*

Alphabetica
Copyright © 2025 by The Estate of Juliet Mattila
All Rights Reserved

No part of this book may be used or reproduced in any manner whatsoever without the prior written permission of both the publisher and the copyright owner.

Book design by Mark E. Cull

Library of Congress Cataloging-in-Publication Data

Names: Mattila, Juliet, 1942–2023 author
Title: Alphabetica : poems / Juliet Mattila.
Description: First edition. | Pasadena, CA : Story Line Press, 2025.
Identifiers: LCCN 2025016873 (print) | LCCN 2025016874 (ebook) | ISBN 9781586541293 paperback | ISBN 9781586541323 library binding | ISBN 9781586541316 epub
Subjects: LCGFT: Poetry
Classification: LCC PS3563.C36587 A78 2025 (print) | LCC PS3563.C36587 (ebook) | DDC 811/.54—dc23/eng/20250410
LC record available at https://lccn.loc.gov/2025016873
LC ebook record available at https://lccn.loc.gov/2025016874

The National Endowment for the Arts, the Los Angeles County Arts Commission, the Ahmanson Foundation, the Dwight Stuart Youth Fund, the Max Factor Family Foundation, the Pasadena Tournament of Roses Foundation, the Pasadena Arts & Culture Commission and the City of Pasadena Cultural Affairs Division, the City of Los Angeles Department of Cultural Affairs, the Audrey & Sydney Irmas Charitable Foundation, the Meta & George Rosenberg Foundation, the Albert and Elaine Borchard Foundation, the Adams Family Foundation, Amazon Literary Partnership, the Sam Francis Foundation, and the Mara W. Breech Foundation partially support Red Hen Press.

First Edition
Published by Story Line Press
an imprint of Red Hen Press
www.redhen.org

ACKNOWLEDGMENTS

Grateful acknowledgment is given to the editors of the publications and journals in which some of these poems first appeared, sometimes in different versions:

Ekphrasis, "In the Dark Manner"; *Flyway*, "Pheasant Stone"; *The Iowa Review*, "Blue," "The Invisible Spectrum"; *Isotope*, "Ectoplasm"; *Neovictorian / Cochlea*, "Muse"; *The Paris Review*, "The Disappearance of the Color Red"; *Passager*, "Tranparence"; *Southwest Review*, "Overcast."

CONTENTS

Alphabetica

Transparence	11
In The Dark Manner	14
Darkness Visible	15
Still Life	16
The Invisible Spectrum	17
Self-Portrait	18
Opposition	19
Midsummer	20
The Messenger	22
Meridian	26
The Disappearance Of The Color Red	30
Living Color	32
Margin	33
Against Lawns	34
Luminato	36
Muse	38
Overcast	39
The Orchard	40
Blue	41
Catch A Falling Star	42
After Noon	44
Ectoplasm	45
Dusk	46

The Unaided Eye	47
As I Flew Out One Morning	48
Interference	50
Night	51
Ink	52
Colorless Green Ideas Sleep Furiously	53
Pheasant Stone	54
The Autobiography Of Music	55
Pheasant	56
Harvest	57
Writing A Life	58
In The Blue Bedroom, Looking Westward	59
MILDRED or *The Book Lover*	63

ALPHABETICA

TRANSPARENCE

As usual the robins returned a full week
before we looked, and (as usual) we feared
crusted snow would undo them. It all melted
down in the mud of a single afternoon when
everything went from zero to sixty just as
fast as robins could fill bare trees with their
grandiose plans. Earth was still brown, and spring seemed
hypothetical (see *Figure 1*—a set of
isosceles triangles that, when assembled
just right should form the maple leaves that won't
kick open until April), and, fearing the worst,
locked inside a down vest (even though the fragrant
murmuring barn was warm) beside the laboring
nannygoat Asphodel, I watched her sides heave and
open wide enough for a membrane to bell out,
push back, then (as she cried) open again and
quickly spill a kid headfirst in the nest of
resilient straw, and after five minutes,
a second. The female is small, trembles, does not
try to stand, cries at the syringe of thick milk I push
under her tongue and spill down my vest . . . Afterwward,
Victor, the youngest horse, touches his enormous
warm nose to the mucus that shines on my clothes and
excites his notice (it is clear, neither white nor
yellow, where we would smell absolutely nothing,
zero) with great interest and restraint.

ADAM COLONIA,
    The Annunciation to the Shepherds

Night and clouds, rendered in fluent
ink around a subtle point where
sky suddenly opens and
a single ray lights an angel's
exploding white curve above
ordinary shepherds: some stand
transfixed, others crawl away
from the scene, escaping,
too frightened to stay or hide
behind their sheep, brown on brown
in the resonant weeds.
Smoke roils over bushes and trees,
returning the eye to the small
white angel,
to the open place in the clouds
through which he blew in a chord
of light. His face is blinding,
so hot Adam obscures it with
the umber that veils the pasture;
his words are music, so piercing
the men he addresses flee
as he arrives, announcing
centuries of blood
and nameless sacrifice,
but Adam paints *wind* in brown
on the grass, and *secret* over
the face of the angel, hides them
even from us. What terror
can we see? The brilliant curved

linen of sudden news
that flattens grass, fells trees?
Or the shadow on the angel's
face, where we look but cannot find
night inside night, a hidden
flame, an imperfection
that, for now, protects us.

IN THE DARK MANNER

From the first state to the seventh,
the etcher slowly darkens his plate,
drawing methodical cross-
hatches in from the edge,
lifting metal
to make night.
Shadows move in from the walls
over soldiers, horses, sheep,
sparing only those
near the lamp.
No proof
is dark enough.
Those he obscures
are still there,
underneath
the lustrous burr:
dice players, merchants,
women weeping into their hands,
trued by the absence
of light.
They stay in the plate
sleeping or turning away
beside the murmuring animals,
but night owns them.
The lamp reveals
the smallest space
around its flame—
even mother and child
begin to vanish.

DARKNESS VISIBLE

Ask it then: by what strange light do we see in dreams?
By the light of the mind, that ultraviolet
chevalier of unreason? Even the most real
dream ends in its own Lethe, its eventual
erasure within the enveloping darkness
from which it came. Our incandescent bodies must
generate a spectral electricity when
hidden in night's dense comforter—a spare phosphor
invisible to others, impartial, a spark
joining the pure flame of desire to the mundane
keepsakes embedded in our memory albums.
Luminous wish! Inevitably touching the
Murmuring dreamer as the light of a star or
Nebula, remembered, brushes sleeping earth.
Or is dream-light a bodiless substance, neither
particle nor wave, not found in textbooks, never
quark nor quantum? One might view dreams as that subtle
rarity, dark matter, breaking onto the bare
sheets as one might break into song, transported and
then gone, as music transpires when past and present
unfasten in performance; or as a form of
virtual travel under the spectral suns of
wildernesses yet undiscovered. Ask Madame
X: *Are dreams the missing mass of the cosmos?* Ask
yourself, ask Nature, ask the wind, who might
zephyr out of the night and divulge the secret.

STILL LIFE

> *Light is the activity of what is transparent.*
> —Aristotle

After dipping a dry brush in water, I stopped,
baffled. I was ten or twelve. I had neither the
courage to choose color nor the wit to say I
did not know which color could represent the tall
elegant glass I'd casually stuffed full of
flowers and placed on crumpled linen. Cosmos and
geraniums were simple—pink and red. But why
had I announced I would paint a still life with flowers
in a voice neither quite off-hand nor meaningful
just as one might declare *I'm going out to play,*
knowing I had no idea how to paint
linen or the aqueous vessel hemmed in its
milky folds? Water made the submerged leaves look quite
numinous, circumscribed by tiny bubbles in
opaque strands, and itself appeared viscous, almost
pond-like in its various reflections, the curved
questions it posed about the shapes that envelop us—
room, window, lamp- containers of radiance. Still
suspended, my brush tried several washes that just
transformed sunlight to mud. Mother walked past and said
Your subject is difficult. Now, I see the glass
vase as only the sum of what it reflected
in water, itself a glaze of images made
explicit on curved pyrex. Then, I felt an un-
yielding flush of anger, not understanding the
ease with which *nature morte* can wear her mirrors.

THE INVISIBLE SPECTRUM

Alpha Centauri is a yellow star. There are
black stars, cut out, backlit, silhouetted against
cobalt after sunset, but how can we see stars
darker than sable wings? Notice, upon slowly
entering a dark room or closet, how linen
folded and laid on shelves envelops every sound
generously, how even light around the door
hesitates, then stops and finally surrenders
in shadows. Just after the last photon ends in
jasmine and the room becomes an invisible
kingdom, it is possible to see black against
lustrous black. The absence of light displaces,
mottles air in an effervescent pattern
near the surface of the eye. The far wall, obscured,
opens, the room empties into the darkness its
poor contents, leaving only the contemplative
quiet of the one color that is no color.
Remember what the thick book of blue-and-white clouds
says: objects will become invisible in the
total absence of earth-light and earth-shine within
unbounded night. In the dark, hands begin to seem
virtual, not real. Open them. They feel almost
weightless, as if pressed against a wall and released,
exalted, like black angels in Flemish paintings,
young, unsmiling, fastened to the pale sky out of
zeal or passion, looking earthward without comment.

SELF-PORTRAIT

        The sun came just as
     I began to say that poppies fade
   in a day—or an hour, if you take them—
and that the hummingbird will never stay,
then the wind turned over its hand and caught
the tarnished silver lens of rain and revealed it, saying
  this way to the far   *shore, take my path*
  in the air beyond   *the sheltering leaves*

OPPOSITION

The color white for many centuries had not one but two opposites: black (as we would expect) and red... Black is somber, red is dense, and white contrasts with both of them.
—Michel Pastoureau

Awake, awake! I started, reached for the alarm—
but it was only a woodpecker, and the noise
continued. Then I understood the woodpecker
drilled on my house. I arose, draped in the faded
elegance of sun, advanced on the continuing
fusillade, opened a window, and marveled at
gallantry in the face of impossible odds:
huge beak, red hairdo, a feathery underside
irresistibly white, like the understory
of the jilted queen's tutu—furiously
knocking, then discarding shreds of brand-new roof trim,
littering the yard with shingles, much as last month's
massive hailstorm had. I, too, was guilty of this;
intent on more light! I'd asked a carpenter to
open skylights in the new roof insurance had
put on to protect my old house until the next
quadrille of shingles stirred up by unexpected
rain-rattling storms. I wondered if the trim was
the sprucewood I'd read about in the Register
that attracted flocks of woodpeckers who hammered
until the walls were lace—our defenses are so
vulnerable. But my siding was asbestos,
weather-worn, neither toxic nor sweet to over-
excited chisel-billed birds. The carpenter said
You'll love this skylight. I do and you do, little
zouave, in your strict uniform of opposites.

MIDSUMMER

What does it mean to think of clouds
tumbled in the gorgeous recitative
of sky?

What does it mean to think of clouds
parsing the wandering sentences of streets?
Let's say

streets turn blue as the bluest sky
after rain (hard, brilliant), after clouds pass.
Let's say

streets become clouds late at night,
milky skeins of mist seining from ditches.
(Remember

stone does not turn to air, outside
the volcano.) Remember sky is not milk,
and that

blue on paper is painted,
and sky is not always blue in its frame
where clouds

divide paint from paper
(can one be made into or out of
the other

if both go unread?)

Is sky all one thought? Can you turn a key
in the wind

as it runs toward you, then pauses,
raveling?—Furious grass, calligraphy
of trees—

Can you make out from this distance
unglossable speech? Difficult explanations?
Fire, then rain—

THE MESSENGER

> *Where is Gabriel*
> *Who was wont to visit my cell?*
> *I call him: Gabriel! He comes not.*
> —Purcell, *Lamentation of the Blessed Virgin*

It is a solitary hour.
Slowly the long day furls into dust.
A girl whose loose hair
darkens her book
leans toward the window, where
the sky studies its calm light.

She turns a page,
and the world pulls.
A flock of birds become black stars,
divertissements of wind;
oh, all day she has turned away
and returned to the still voice
of the book.

Outside the sound of wings,
linen ripping the air.
A fan flares out of a closed hand,
fills into the shape of a man.
She turns toward the sound,

turns where he stands in the door
and steps in, arm outstretched.
The air shimmers

around a green stem
bowed by the unpronounceable weight
of lilies.

The man wears a musical speech
of linen, blue
as the shadow of trees on snow.
An etude of silk works its rill
down the sleeve.
His hand trembles. White trumpets
spend their bright dust.

Then he speaks to her, says her name.
It does not sound like her name,
and her pulse slips, quicksilver,
when she answers, here I am.
Heat quivers at his wings.
He speaks in a strange voice,
a man from across the sea.

He says breast, belly, spill.
He says womb, says she will come
to the mossy pith of blood,
smiling as though he knows
the delight of touching her.

For a long time
he does not speak,
but sings.
She sees his red and green

eye, iris of desire,
each black lash
shining perfectly,
forgets herself.
Her heart is wax,
the room throbs,
a mirror loose
on its wall.

He stays with her
for an hour,
then leaves,
a hem in the wind.

Could it have been an hour?
The sky still light,
the men not returned,
birds walking
in the shocked and dusty road?

No feather or imprint
on the impassive stone.
Only the lilies, flung across a chair,
softening to skin.
Their thick perfume
stuns the room.

A loss of words.
Exile to a land

where no one speaks.
She sees herself with wings,
asleep, wrapped in wings.

She walks to the door
where he revealed himself,
clothed in the sane light
of the room,
clothed in the cricket's shrill
afternoon drone.

Will she find him there,
by the stone
where the fence meets the tree?
There, in the cloud of bees
stirring fallen fruit
on the ground?

Has he left her here
so she will find him everywhere?
When will she see her house,
its walls, its sweet fountain,
unaltered?
And if the house stands firm,
then she herself is lost,
and who will want her?

She wants him here again,
this way: two sheaves of wheat
curved in the arm of a harvester.

MERIDIAN

(Orpheus and Eurydice)

Is she there,
dark vein in marble,
walking? Where is
the curve of rib and arm
in the sightless night?
O held breath,
there is no light
to find a path.

Midnight below,
noon above.

He wants to bind her
to his side.
He walks ahead.
She is a plant, green
at the root.
Can she return,
breaking through snow,
the long winter
forgotten?

She looks back:
a featureless plain,
marriage to the land
of silk and veins,
the custom
of feeling nothing.

She is a secet.
He wants her
to step from his mind
into the grass and moving air
of the world. He wants
to draw an invisible
landscape of hours,
devise an unfamiliar day.

What is a dream?
(her soundless face)
What, then is life?
(household at peace,
fertile harvest)—
less vivid dreams?

She sees a ruined wall.
Light blooms beyond
the last curve.

Night within night,
invisible dark.

Can they live
in our world of unhoused
iron and grief?
How dear is unlived life?
Will he lose all he has
and all he does not have?

Unmade design,
untasted hours.

Let history stop.
Let them walk in desire
in the middle of life,
not turning back
before he turns,
before he sees
not her
but the world without her—
cold spring, drought, famine—
before he begs trees
and stones for comfort,
before he pays for song
with his own blood,
before she returns
to night, can history wait?

Still wind,
hidden truth.

Let him know her step,
the leap of her heart,
without sight.

Let him find her long stem,
her powerful bloom,
without scent.

Let him graze the skin
of her arm, her trailing dress
without touch.

Let him drink the clear air
of her voice
without taste.

Let him open the charm
of her name
without sound.

Let the work of the senses
pass from art
into faith.

THE DISAPPEARANCE OF THE COLOR RED

for John Ash

The middle ages had ended
even in the provinces,
but at first no one noticed
that apples stayed green,
and the juice of pomegranates ran brown.

After winter, the red mines closed.
The words, crimson, scarlet, vermillion
passed from common use,
and poets began to praise
ochre lips, amber cheeks.

Bureaucrats cast off their official hats
(tall crimson cylinders)
and no could paint the cardinal
save with a kind of umber
milled from certain ores

that taste flat (when the tongue
touches the manuscript)
as the modest cereals
that sustained entire garrisons
through years of siege.

No cochineal, no grenadine, no lake.
Did no one notice?
Or were the literati so distraught
they could not bear to enter it
in their otherwise ample chronicles?

Times were hard. Vessels
exhumed from the ruined capitol
hid their pallor
with a brackish glaze,
as if part of the visible spectrum

had vanished, as if the rose clay
from which they were pulled—
a pinch, followed by a blush—
had drained back into the earth
with the wine it once held.

LIVING COLOR

August, the Fifties. My father looks up from his
book (Plato) to ask why on earth am I using
color film to take pictures of a black-and-white
dog? It isn't cost that worries him, color more
expensive than monochrome; it's just another
fusillade in his war against redundancy,
geopolitics of the lawn chair. I explain
hastily that photographing a spotted dog
in color, in summer, say, near a river, or
just beneath a tree, makes white natural, lends a
kind of distinction lacking in a black-and-white
landscape where the dog could be lost, overwhelmed by
middle grays—even though I understand this is
not his point. There is no river here, he says. His
open book dazzles. How can he read that blazing
page in the sun? On the sidewalk, maple branches
quickly project a moving tree. So few things
are ever black or white—on grass, the maple's shade
slips imperceptibly from watered-down sable
to green—as for the dog, what color he was
under the tree, I can't say, exactly. He was
vital, a blur, but in our world of traffic, he
would not be that for long. Today the bruised fragrance
exhaled by clover, sweet, humid, brings me back to
yesterday, my father, the foolish dog—back to
the zenith, noon, where shadows write, erase, rewrite.

MARGIN

Once by the ocean I disturbed a swamp
of rainwater caught in ancient granite
where dragonflies scribbled their arabesques,
whirring cellophane taut over black net.
Who first called them devil's darning needles
and mistook them for steel, fettered by silk
to its broken measure? Ancient experts
of weeds and sedge at the pond's meniscus,
dragonflies dart like thought: absolute speed
to absolute stillness, then to wind again,
shining. Can needles zigzag the torn edge
of water to its reeds? Think of stirring
dry leaves (silk sleeves in the wind). Think of life
on the wing, untied, carrying nothing . . .

AGAINST LAWNS

for Ed and Pat Folsom

All of them, whether timothy or zoysia
(because meadows are no longer scythed by slaves or
chewed by cows), must be mowed. At first, dandelions
distemper a fair field, then plantain overruns
emerald intensity, ravishing the thin
fabric of a beauty so fragile that one English
grandee glimpsed it only when drawn in a swift and
handsome coach on a smooth turf, with graduated
inclines and declivities—praising the shaven
jade of lawns in terms of the very wheels that would
kill them. Ease and speed—a short drive to the clover-
leaf, the thundering freeway. Oh, grass can appear
miraculous after drought, or a hard winter
near the sullen Ides, when it recovers greenness
overnight and morphs straw into chartreuse through no
power greater than the migrant sun's radiant
quanta; parks and clearings roll out their illusions,
revelations of velvet that protect us from
surrounding wilderness by opening vistas,
then dissolving them into luminous distance,
unearthly air. But wilderness waits, counting its
violent thistles. Ask the old laureate of grass,
Walt, whether he finds God's handkerchief dropt in our
xeriscape of shopping malls and asphalt. His great
yawp was not about you, lawns, your taste for
zillions of precious gallons, but about wind

zithering though big bluestem, the complicated
yammer of grasslands about to be ploughed into
extravagant dust, into theory. The six-foot
woven grass of the prairie (unutterable,
voluminous, shuttled by air, by a thickened
understory of roots, resilient meristem
trim in shadow, wild oats, switch grass, Indian grass)
survives only in the late book of our fateful
rondure, plant collections of herbariums or
quiet cemetery where the uncut hair of graves
persists, revealing the dusty end of the
open road, the battlefields where earth repays our
numberless dead with the largesse of untended
meadows. But this is all a dream, it blew away
long ago, and the wilderness waits, tying its
knotted highways. Although I admit some private
joy pushing a mower from curb to shining curb,
inscribing squares and triangles to decorate
the humid carpet of memory, I think of Persian
gardens where bare stones support the mirages of
flying carpets laid ravishingly upon them.
Even when weeding, I know the man in gray flannel
deserves his Eden, but then I drop the trowel,
close my eyes and see weeds, medicated grass, the
betrayal of cement, and I am against lawns,
against their unsustainable consolation.

LUMINATO

After Lorrain

Morning after morning
he slips from my side
and goes alone to the clearing,
to capture aspects of sun
on an unsettled
curtain of trees.

His hand's bravura
is all instinct.
He cannot restrain
the wind he summons
to fill the leaves,
or the sun he clothes
in shimmering washes
of grey and ox-gall.

Light is his only love,
her brief caresses,
her intimate emanations.
He unfastens gates
and unlaces meadows,
after the perfume
of saturated azure,
the meridian's
invisible elation.

Her glancing touch
on hills and fields,
her vapory adieus,
are more present in his mind
when he returns
than the flickering lamp
in the inn where I wait.
He takes my hand
(veiled in a cloud of fragrance)
and kisses it, for a moment.

MUSE

Like old men who fall asleep with the Aeneid
(well, quite unlike) I fell asleep over Celan
last night, then stumbled up to extinguish lights
hours later. The house held a dank chill, perhaps
because the cold earth had absorbed all the light
that poured so thoughtlessly from open windows.
As I darkened each room, new words entered my mind—
a faraway Quasar completed its circuit,
or the voice of Celan separated itself
from the electrons that surround us every night.
I have had too many dreams of the perfect phrase
or line, and have repeated them too many times
so as never to forget, and then awakened
without evidence (not a stain on the pillow)
of how words explain us and everything else.
Still in the momentary pause after the faint
hum of light stopped and silence occupied
its absence, new words opened in incomparable
black, the sable of an acre of plowed earth after
burning. Was it some god entering a thought?
Or a power of sleep reaching to transform ordinary
words into something a few can open?

OVERCAST

At the present moment how much gray have we got?
Let's promote gray for everything.
    —Diana Vreeland

Actually, the problem with most clouds is that
(for better or worse) they have no story—not in
the commonly accepted sense of a progress,
diagonal or straight, from beginning through middle
to end, where a small but telling epiphany
flares out as though "meaning" could compensate for the sky's
graceless disorder. What is success, to a cloud?
Holding entire Adirondacks prisoner behind
intangible veils? When the last vapors disperse,
the jailer vanishes, restoring all of those
kidnapped stones to their settings without threatening
letters or ransom notes. What effect does never
mind have on the reader of the sky's unending
narration? Clouds begin, and begin again, as though
once upon a time were the whole story. One thinks
particularly of February, when they
quilt over our thrilling sky with 'dark white,' and then
reject the idea of progress, replaying
the same chord every day, lowering the ceiling,
turning down the lights, returning the sun's bright gifts
unopened. They work behind the scenes while concealing
virtually nothing about themselves. Call them
weeping concrete or what you will (not dove, not pearl),
this excess of gray is like the talker who makes us
yearn for a shapely story with an ending not
zinc, not lead, not ash, not dust, not obscured by

THE ORCHARD

After the thunderstorm, a small white cloud of mist
breathed out of the wetlands and assembled itself
coolly in the meadow. It was a piece torn from
the disordered clouds that crashed and sped furiously
east: a pent-up sigh from the earth's waterlogged
fundament, let out like the sun after the storm's
gray winds pushed aside trees to get their way. The mist
hung like a glittering idea over the grass,
as incandescent beneath the rinsed sun as the
jeweled ropes and swags of a chandelier. Oh, I
knew there had to be a rainbow inside, but the
laws of light made it invisible; no one, no
matter how keen-eyed, could see it without standing
knee-deep in the sullen swamp. (As rainbows are not
objects, they are not there if no one can see them, but
perversely they are not nothing.) In front of our
quiet house, flashing lights drew up, red, blue, yellow,
to remove a maple shattered across the road.
Sheer elation at the sustenance of light had held
the rotten trunk. It was hauled off in chains and laid
under the apple trees, where pools of rainwater,
vividly reflecting the last light of the sky
in watery regard, sank down into the earth
and were exhaled from the grass as the first fireflies,
yellow, signaling, drifting effortlessly down,
inscribing slow arcs beneath ancient branches.

BLUE

All day, the overcast ended just west of here.
Beyond the far field we could see a featureless
cerulean, out of reach and perfect, without
depth, tantalizing us with the indifference of
eternal sunlight on a day surrendered to
fulminant gray. Normally, sky above far hills
(gauzy dust and elements blurring the humid
horizon) is not blue or gray, but rose bleeding
into gold or perhaps green. To name the hue of this
jumble of elements, particles, the subtle
kinetic veil left hanging after factories
lock up and call it a day, gaze upward at the
meridian fixedly to define azure,
noticing how full and empty it is, how it
opens and limits us, a definition that's
paradoxical. Then glance at the horizon
quickly to learn the color it offers up as
relief from incessant blue. As a spectacled
shy child who preferred reading to baseball, I would
throw myself in the clover of left field and look
until I felt myself begin to fall up—not
vertigo—a drop into emptiness, unlike
wind or water, but thrilling nonetheless. You are
excessively serious, my teacher said, and
you never smile—but of course, one cannot see the
zenith of stars obscured by thin, unclouded air.

CATCH A FALLING STAR

America, not singing or making money,
but painted from sea to shining sea by Midwest
children on their school playground, in the peculiar
different colors used for maps (what held my
eye was the unnamed capitals, each marked by a black
five-painted star); America, you caught me off-
guard on the cold asphalt of an overcast day
halfway through winter, caught me out walking, with the
innocence of your pastel paint. I'd escaped the
jumble of dead plaster and woodwork in the blue
kitchen of the old house I'd bought, sulking; I was
laughably broke, could not remodel, but just then
a mysterious scrap of paper blew out of a
nearby dumpster and landed at my feet. I leaned
over; it was the stencil of the star used to
paint all the state capitals on that map! It went
quickly into my pocket. Flying stencils are
rare! They're omens, they can give you ideas! Next
stop: the hardware store. I'd never defaced walls, nor
tried graffiti, but reaching out for a spray can of
undiluted jonquil, I thought this might be the
very time Jiminy Cricket had predicted
to wish upon—or better, to distemper the
exhausted cerulean of my kitchen with—
yellow stars, frescoed particulars of the old
zodiac that endures beyond falling plaster or

atomic wiring. Should I do this? I wondered
back in the kitchen. Will this yellow enamel
confer a certain je ne sais quoi on the per-
durable metal bolted to the wall in an
emergency (a galvanized cicatrix of
Frankenstein-like ingenuity) to conceal the
grisly remains of nameless plumbing disasters?
Here I paused, looking around at the walls covered with
invidious scrawls of black mastic laid by some
juiced-up abstract expressionist intent on
keeping up with the Joneses by gluing stylish
linoleum so tightly it could never be
moved—until later it was removed, leaving a
noxious stickum behind. I pushed the button.
Out sprayed a scintillating ray of cadmium's
power and magic, and though I moved the stencil
quickly from place to place on the plaster, yellow
ran partway down the wall, overflowing the arms
of several stars. Eventually a man would
trowel over the mastic, burying my stars
under layers of white (I still see them in my mind's
vision, taking in the ladder, the spray can. Do you
expect ever to sell this house? he asked. Because
you've just lowered its value quite a lot. It's not
zero yet, he added, trying to be helpful.

AFTER NOON

When the day calls us
to her old heart,
when the sun slips
past our trees,
how late is it?
                Think
of each day as a blank
canvas, perfect
and terrible.
Dusk thickens
around us.
This is the edge

of the world.
Tomorrow is here
and the next day.
My linen dress
burns like a poppy.

ECTOPLASM

A cloudless word, *fluorescence.* Memories of summer
back in the years when television was new, when
counterinsurgency sprays had not yet been
directed against insects or the rest of us;
evenings, then, were our late arenas, where we ran
far across neighboring lawns, florid in after-
glow, unsupervised until parents called. I spent
hours and hours swerving through twilight pursuing
illumination, commandeering old Mason
jars to catching lightning bugs for our next-door neighbor,
a quiet man investigating sources of cold
light for the Navy. As night overcame the sky,
millions of fireflies sparked and rose up from the grass,
now blazing, now dark, moving invisibly and
obliquely out of sight. Salary: one penny
per beetle. It took thousands to research the trick
question of how they bring lust to light without heat.
Running back and forth in the spacious dusk, I would
slide a pale hand behind slow wings and then *seize it!*
They tingled like my feet when I peered into the
unreal fluoroscope at the shoe store, saw dark bones
verified inside green toes, green shoes. Then someone
wrote up the dangers of imaging young feet with
X-rays, and the machines vanished, as would, after
years of spraying our endless waves of grain, all those
zigzagging fireflies, and night returned to the stars.

DUSK

After you left
I had nothing to wear.
Rain, some pollen.

I reached into your letter
and took out a word
which resembled

night sky
draped over my
skin,

and I remembered
how you dressed me
with your hands.

THE UNAIDED EYE

Accident, or what passes for it, destiny,
blows me into the pedestrian mall, our town's
concrete remedy for urban decay, one cold
December evening. Late for a meeting, I've
elected to walk, but have to run, then finally
fly through a red light and nearly collide with
gears and drives and polyvinyl tubes—a giant
homemade telescope that a man has assembled,
inviting those who cross the recycled bricks set
jewel-like underfoot to look through a billion
kilometers of space at planets beyond our
local rush of atoms. Impervious to strange
men, I nonetheless stop and find Saturn in his
numberless rings trembling in the telescope's
open eye. Moved by opportunity or just
plain luck, meeting forgotten, I cross into the
quadrant of night where Jupiter travels, hardly
red or sanguine, but ivory with pale brown streaks,
stains that won't wash out. I tell the astronomer
there is no red there. The eye isn't able to
understand incandescent gas, the man says; film
virtualizes the "red." I look up to find
white-blue, but I still want the Great Red Spot to look
exactly as in books: fevered, not washed out by
years of space. I want to open your colors, 0
Zodiac! its gifts undiminished by distance.

AS I FLEW OUT ONE MORNING

Apollo landed beside me in seat sixteen-
B out of Chicago. Grasping my traveling
charm (winged horse rampant on ancient Athenian
drachm) I watched him furtively search the seat, perhaps
eager to retrieve his coin, or simply groping
for the end of his seat belt, inadvertently
girdling my hips with its promise of safety.
He drew back, embarrassed: *I thought I'd scared you off.*
I thought of Daphne dismantling herself, rough-hewn,
just as his arms closed in, a vision of leafy
kindling preferable to being loved and then
left. But I was not a tree, and he was not white
marble, he was black, glittering with a kind of
numinous dew, so young, and I could hardly run
off, sewn as we both were deep in the air-
plane. When Apollo said he was an actor, so
quietly that all the blessed clouds outside us
reddened, I saw we were birds flying through the pink
smog that tempts Detroit, far below, with the perfumed
taste of its cruel sunset. Soldiering paid for his
unfinished life—dance, plucked heartstrings—even erased
the veil of race, kept in reserve for the next oil
war in the desert. Not the education he
expected, replacing his theatre tour of
Yale with the echoing empty house of Az-
Z—, where he believed his company would be

assigned. He paused. I saw our lives as flecks of foam
borne up by the larger wave, out of the rocking
cradle, luminous, practical, then casually
dispersed—as the plane descended toward darkling
earth. Without self-pity he described his chances:
far from the front, still a target, safe as any
good American ever is. As we fall from
heaven, imagine, when beacons call passengers
inward at evening on aluminum wings, this
jeu de theatre: reverse the film, undo Ovid,
knead rough bark into skin, tree back to woman, comb
laurel boughs back to graying hair, so I might place
my leafy hand over Apollo's beating heart,
needing to comfort, as any mother does (his
own had passed); but I see he is already too
profoundly encircled: by the seat belt, the steep
queue of planes spiraling earthward, the luminous
room in which we are privileged to fly, by the
essential indenture of class, which has let him
underwrite his life—still under construction . . .

> *Long, too long, America,*
> *Traveling roads all even and peaceful you learn'd from*
>   *joys and prosperity only,*
> *But now, ah now, to learn from crises of anguish, advancing,*
>   *grappling with direst fate and recoiling not,*
> *And now to conceive and show to the world what your*
>   *children en-masse really are . . .*
>   —Walt Whitman, *Drum-Taps*

INTERFERENCE

Almost everyone fails to notice the battered
brown television set and castaway milk
crates stashed next to the formal garden of the Art
Deco townhouse, left in plain sight week after week,
encroaching on a line of gilded wrought-iron
fence posts that protect its shiny green
garden from both house and street. Most nights at dusk a
homeless man shows up and jimmies an otherwise
invisible door at the base of the streetlight,
joining the television's trailing wires with a
kinetic splice to the current flowing inside
the lamppost with electrical tape and enough
manual dexterity to outmaneuver
the nasty shock that lies in wait for those who stand
on earth. The screen fills with static as the man
places his TV tenderly on one milk crate, then
quickly pulls up another and sits two feet from
rolling snow, staring intently at a tuneless
storm of electrons spilling over jokes and laugh
track, oblivious to passers-by. Late at night,
unencumbered by shopping cart or bags, he'll
vanish after hours of parsing images from
the white noise of hyperkinetic electrons,
expertly disconnected, not homeless perhaps,
yet living off the grid in some refuge where his
zeal to pull images from air is not indulged.

NIGHT

Poised to write
about the color *blue*
I wrote your name
on the empty sheet.

What was I thinking
when I wrote your name
in the strange light
of thunderheads?

All night,
the noise of rain.
All night your name
against my cheek.

INK

> *The manuscript has the aspect of a battlefield on which each inch of forward momentum has been wrested at exorbitant human cost from an implacable enemy.*
> —Judith Thurman

About halfway through the file of my life,
behind an old folder marked "Art," I found
a crumpled typescript, erased, retyped, erased—smudged
dark as an old etching. I quickly recognized
every letter of my old typewriter, but I
failed to remember the text itself. Where had I
gotten this? I wondered (the few poems that others
had lathered themselves up to present to me were
indelibly inscribed within my memory,
jangling with the times tables and my first
kiss and the names of all the cats I'd ever met).
Leafing from page to page, I uncovered a far
more devastated handwritten draft with the same
name as the typed version, each word crossed out
obliterated, at least once. Entire sentences,
phrases (like as all just a dream had vanished
quite beyond) recall down the black *oubliette* of
reconsidered lines. The writing was mine, the ink
sable, Permanent India used (I was so
terribly young) because it was waterproof. What
unanticipated tears and rainstorms had been
vanquished, what UV rays warded off, as I un-
wrote the long page! Fortunately, some small portions not
X-ed endured (silence is not the perfect un-
yielding poem), had been rescued in typescript. Freed from
zero, but not from the oblivion of ink.

COLORLESS GREEN IDEAS SLEEP FURIOUSLY

for Noam Chomsky

after a thunderstorm spends itself, leaving torn
branches strewn over harrowing asphalt. After
campanula and several plants of the meadow,
doronicum and achillea, root themselves
effortlessly in ancient stone walls assembled
famously without mortar. After 'camelopard,'
'griffon,' and 'unicorn' gather below a small
hill in Paradise where Adam, pointing in all
innocence, names the animals in a frescoed
jardin, an Eden barely verdant, where each
kind of animal is drawn patiently upon
luminous gray ground. Unobserved, the serpent has
moved forward, underneath an elephant's upraised
neutral foot—eager to shrink the garden to an
oblique green thought—and the elephant looks at us,
prepared to stop him. Should he? One answer to this
question comes in the form of intelligent new
roses whose fragrance goes beyond gardenia and
stephanotis—after lichen-covered rocks un-
tangle extreme rivers. Colorless green ideas
(unquiet) do sleep furiously after
verdant temple roofs of laurel leaves wither to
wax and feathers, then to patinated brass—an
experiment confirmed by two references in
yesterday's papers. After Adam christens the
'zebra,' who steps from long grass into black and white.

PHEASANT STONE

That morning, he had eaten grass, feed corn scattered
near the barn for cattle, and the seed of smartweed.
I find them whole, hours later, a thick mash
kneaded inside his crop's pearly membrane.
One touch of the knife parts it like a curtain
drawn aside to reveal the events of a winter day,
sunny, food everywhere, not too cold,
a day he moved from field to woods and back to field.
The blue and scarlet gizzard proves more difficult,
clenched around its abrasive grit. I cut until
the convex striated wall of muscle opens
to reveal a rock about the size of a bean.

Even the smallest field stones are too large to swallow.
He must have found this in the sand beside the road.
Muddy brown quartz, it had not, like other rocks,
been squeezed into dust. Some people think pheasant stones
are special, but a pheasant's amber eye, even half-
closed in its limp head, is more striking. If I put
this small dull stone in my pocket, how soon will I
forget what I've found. Better to let it drop
in the grass and let earth recover it, so
it may be chosen again, in some other way.

THE AUTOBIOGRAPHY OF MUSIC

Like wings, I begin and end in stillness.
Like wind, I am neither here nor there.
Like water, I run past and disappear.
Like a heart, I cry out beneath your hand.

PHEASANT

After the others
scare us, bursting
into the wind,
you stop the sleigh.
The horses rear
and plunge, remembering
wings, wanting
us to be lighter than air.
The dog hears her under the snow.
I run to the drift
before he can lift her.
She is light.
She has closed her eyes.
Before you say, *throw her
over the fence!*
she disappears,
leaving my fingers
covered with feathers.

HARVEST

From a hill
where deer leave
their curved tracks,
I watch fences
and trees.
Men raise their guns.
The sound is small
in the enormous air.
Birds flash
from the leaves
and the wind moves on
down the rows
to a quiet place
in the grass
(a hand placed
over the eyes)
where breath goes on
for a time
and the dog works to find
a beating wing.

WRITING A LIFE

for Langdon Hammer and Uta Gosmann

The last distortion of romance
Forsook the insatiable egotist.
   —Wallace Stevens

And they all lived happily ever after—or
better yet, *unhappily.* Our small lives must lack
closure as we improvise them? Even after
Death gives the Maiden her first real kiss, numerous
enigmas linger behind, eddying in her
fragrant wake—lost when transcribed in the partial
grammar of memory. If we draw a line from
here to there in late afternoon, when slanted rays
illuminate lintels and hallways, we can still
justify looking backward to search for dropped hand-
kerchiefs, trails of crumbs, the odd footprint. How should we
look to the past? Not like History's Angel, poised to
moralize the rush of debris accumulating
near her feet. It takes courage not to point out the
obvious lessons when lives end unfinished, though
parables advise otherwise. What inscrutable
quantum theory might expose the conversion of
"Real Life" to fable? We should forgive the fluid
self as simply change in permanence, a rainbow
tentative over gravity. Who says *'Je' est*
un autre will ignite an unstable mix of
vision and desire—oil shimmering on asphalt—
when love attempts to ghostwrite its entrances and
exits. Every lived life, dutiful even in
youth, maturing neither wholly in diamond or
zircon, stays unfixed—until, in fact, it vanishes.

IN THE BLUE BEDROOM, LOOKING WESTWARD

Angelica has mastered *drag* and *drop*.
Braiding my hands behind her broad back, I
cannot lose her, as she whirls me in a
dizzying waltz from bed to chair. A rare
evening sky of dense violet unfurls
far above the mountains in silent but
grateful acknowledgment that gravity
has not yet accounted for every thing
artistic license grants our earthly rounds.
Just imagine that we saw no sunsets
kindling clouded images in the west!
Lacking that, how would my lifelong waltz end?
Moiled in a sweaty heap on the dance floor or
noisome parterre, with my exhausted dance
partner left gasping after the startled
quiet of the orchestra, its final
rhythmic pulse done. Angels dance so
serenely on the heads of pins, spinning
timelessly. Don't drop me, Angelica,
unless it's the right time for my transient
vivid heart to pause for the moment,
exhale, and sigh farewell, as you make rounds.
We all fall down. Nevertheless, in spite of that, we must
yearn not to become ashes of roses,
zodiac dust, shadows, echoes, ectoplasm.

MILDRED

or

The Book-Lover

MILDRED
or
The Book Lover

for Richard Howard

Of the part of my life
before I came to the bookstore
there is little to say.
These days, I prefer
not think of it.

My new life began
the day I settled into a chair
in the store window.
So many of us can trace
a change in our lives
to a turned page,
a new leaf.

I could *read* in the city!
Books would be my trees,
my vines, my running brooks!
The chair embraced me
like an old shawl.
I picked up a volume,
something about Calculus
or Catullus,

opened it, and began to read
right there in the bookstore
as everyone watched.
When the Book of Life opens,
our readings are not secret,

but it felt private, somehow,
in the shop window. I sat
alone with the audible voice
of the past—not my past,
mind you, that was over—
but the words of a dream
in my ear.

It may be a fine thing
to start life with a few
great books of one's own,
but I had no books
aside from Nature,
and no taste for the games
my family played
with food or lice.
I was always dreaming,
abstracted and dawdling
on the daily sweep
through the treetops.

I thought of my sisters
confined in small rooms
pounding typewriters,
racing against time
to rewrite Shakespeare,
my brothers in laboratories,
infected with AIDS
or wedged in capsules
flaming to the moon,
and the caged chimps
taught to speak
with their hands—
prisoners, all of them.

But I—I was free!
I could read!

My version of wings
was a book
where I could study
human pursuits,
the baffling cousins
a few helices away.
To my mind, each book
holds a fixed place
in the chain of being,
like a plant or mineral.

The light in the bookstore
was fluorescent until ten,
when a resinous
blue neon sign
made "TEXTBOOKS"
flame in the night,
and I could roam
the darkened store,
liberating one or two
from their snug shelves:
Proust, Trollope, Robbe-Grillet,
The Farmer's Almanac,
even the *OED,* stunning
in the sheer casualness
of its matter.

Fifteen years passed,
five thousand nights
without a flashlight—
and before I knew it,

I had read my eyes out.
One fell off and was lost,
leaving a small brown
hollow in my fur
and a small hole
where it had been sewn;
the other hung by a thread.

Like books, we have our fortunes,
lucky or unlucky
in the precise moment
they befall us.
One night in the blue window,
I sat trying to read
The Decline of the West
with my good eye,
but like those women
perched in neon windows
to show what they can do,
I had grown notorious.
All the world knew me
in my bookstore
and a man wanted me.

Not for the carelessness
of my dishabille or lace
(if Macaulay, with his
occasional flashes of silence
was "like a book in breeches,"
what would my uncut
silence be? "A book in furs?"
Slipcovered in the jingling
silence of a sleigh, gliding
over Arctic snow?

Oh, I know about fur-
covered teacups and plates,
but there are no books with pelts;
I've only seen one,
a domestic novel
of denning bears,
nothing about Venus,
or beauty bare.)

—But I digress,
filled with the sunshine
of my work.
Perhaps he loved me
for my plush—not scarlet,
but Victorian nevertheless.

The bookstore refused
to give their consent,
but the man was insistent,
even ardent. Years passed;
he continued to visit.
When the bookstore closed,
I was for sale
with the other fixtures
and the man bought me.
I don't know what drew
his heart; was it that
I worked harder than he
to absorb letters? That
I never took notes?
Or that alone at night
I preferred a book in the hand
to other comforts? After all,

where is human nature weaker
than in a bookstore?

First things first, the man said
(sweeping me off my feet).
I want to take you shopping.
We sped to the Doll Hospital.
Six dollars and fifty cents later,
I had a pair of shining eyes,
tightly sewn. I could see
far better than before,

so when he threw open his door
and carried me over the threshold
of Apartment 5X,
all I saw were *books, books, books!*
Stacked in shelves
from floor to ceiling,
over windows and doors,
down halls. . .
No moveables to speak of,
a chair here and there,
Turkish carpets flung carelessly,
their transports not needed,
—no furniture so charming
as books. *What's mine
is yours,* he said,
wanting to broaden my horizons, to show me
his small Utopia,
where no barriers of sense
impede the grace
of print. We all know
stories belong
to the eyes that see them.

That day,
I read no more,
but climbed from shelf to shelf
scanning the titles—
his very walls a map
of old obsessions,
his taste somewhat obscure,
no shelf space wasted.
I felt utterly at home
in his clear, brown, twilit
atmosphere of words.

Toward evening, the inevitable
question arose
of sleeping arrangements.
There was only one bed
(little more than a cot)
tucked in a sweet
sequestered nook,
held up by a matched set
of Balzac, in red Morocco,
where he made room for me
at one end.

Oh, exquisite reader,
my double, my sister,
I could not marry him.
I am no demi-rep
that loves, but saves her soul
with French romance.
As I read all night,
I sit at his feet,
anchoring his dreams
in which his dear books

sing to him, ventriloquy
that only he can hear.
Each volume I long for
in the lustrous dark
comes to hand:
the Book of Nature,
knitted up with secrets;
the Book of Logic,
blotted over with tears;
the Book of Knowledge
with many blank pages;
the Book of Love,
written by no one;
the Book of the Universe,
inscribed in circles;
the Book of Life, which begins
with two creatures
in a library.

You understand
that books do not think for me.
The Book of Fate
I leave unopened,
but I do know,
in the gray volume of my brain,
that his books and my heart
must never part,
and that I will never cry
The flesh is sad, alas!
Or *I have read all his books.*

BIOGRAPHICAL NOTE

Born 1942 in Fargo, ND, Juliet Mattila received a BA and MA from the University of California at Berkeley, a PhD from the University of Chicago, and an MFA from the University of Iowa. While in Chicago, she worked on and served as editor in chief of *The Chicago Review*. She taught English at Loyola University of Chicago (1968–71) and at the University of Rochester (1971–6) before directing the Academic Advising Center at the University of Iowa (1982–2000). Her poems, essays, and reviews appeared in a variety of periodicals and anthologies, including *The Yale Review*, *The Paris Review*, *Studies in English Literature*, and *Isotope*. Several of her radio plays were performed on the Iowa Radio Project, which aired on fifty NPR stations (1992). Both a prize-winning poet and photographer, she died at her home in Santa Fe, July 19, 2023.

www.ingramcontent.com/pod-product-compliance
Lightning Source LLC
Chambersburg PA
CBHW030913170426
43193CB00009BA/833